ZIMBABWE PORTRAIT ZIMBABWE PORTRAIT ZIMBABWE PORTRAIT ZIMBABWE PORTRAIT ZIMBABWE PORTRAIT ZIMBABWE PORTRAIT ZIMBABWE PORTRAIT

ZIMBABWE PORTRAIT

Compiled by

Dick Pitman

Compiled and written by Dick
Pitman and published by Clive
Murphy of Modus Publications
(Pvt) Ltd., P O Box 66070,
Kopje, Harare, Zimbabwe.

ISBN 0-7974-0725-1

Set in Triplet Light Italic by
Modus Publications (Pvt) Ltd.
Originated by Print Originators
and printed on 105 gsm Everest Cartridge
by National Printing and Packaging

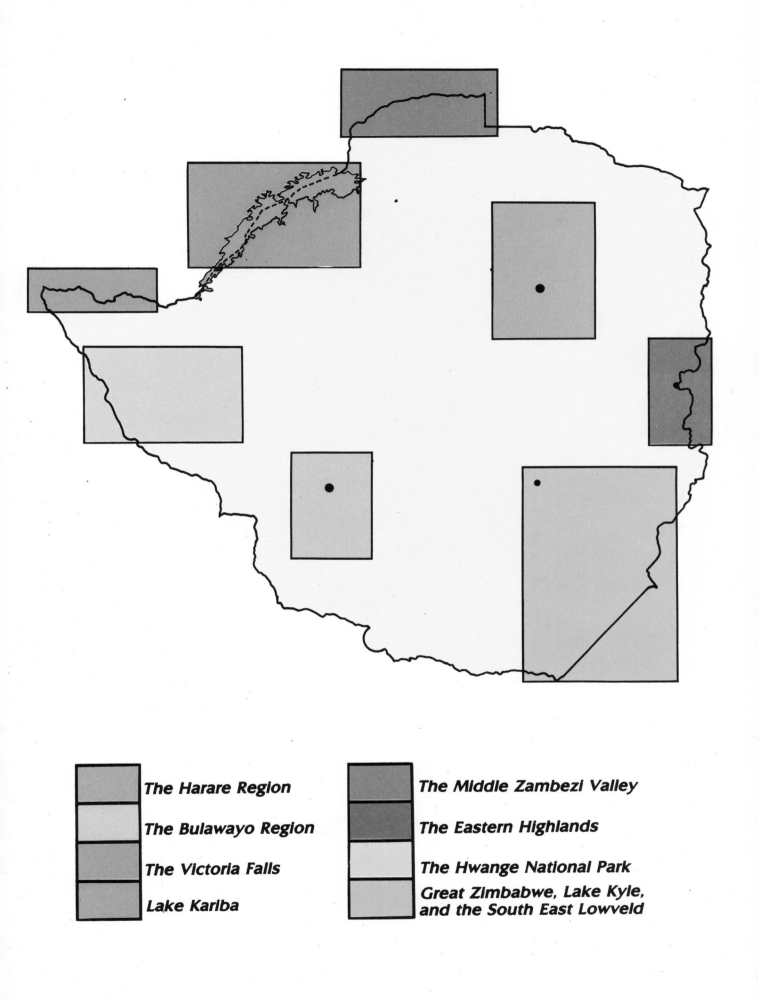

The Harare Region

The Bulawayo Region

The Victoria Falls

Lake Kariba

The Middle Zambezi Valley

The Eastern Highlands

The Hwange National Park

Great Zimbabwe, Lake Kyle,
and the South East Lowveld

WHAT IS a portrait? It may be photographic in its detail, or eloquent in its simplicity, but its purpose is to bring forth the essential characteristics that sum up a face, a landscape — or a country.

ZIMBABWE PORTRAIT is not a reference book. It is an armchair journey through the landscapes and cities of a beautiful country, to be picked up or put down at leisure.

It has been compiled from material used over many years in publications such as Africa Calls, In Flight and Zimbabwe Wildlife. Such material is often used once, then left to lie forgotten when in fact it deserves a far wider audience.

It has been my pleasure to take this material — which, at one time or another, has dealt with most aspects of Zimbabwe life — and to piece it together into a larger picture.

The brush strokes in ZIMBABWE PORTRAIT are the immense spaces of Hwange, the loveliness of Kariba, Mana Pools and our other wild places, lightly overlaid with man's imprint in the form of our history, our agriculture and our cities.

Readers will find a certain emphasis on the conservation of Zimbabwe's scenery and wildlife. Surely, in the long term, nothing can be more important than the quality of the world we inhabit — and few crimes more heinous than its unthinking destruction.

ZIMBABWE PORTRAIT will certainly age with the years; but I trust that the beauty it portrays will not.

The Victoria Falls

The Hwange National Park

Lake Kariba

The Middle Zambezi Valley

The Harare Region

The Bulawayo Region

Great Zimbabwe, Lake Kyle and the South East Lowveld

The Eastern Highlands

The Victoria Falls

"Scenes so lovely must have been gazed upon by angels in their flight."
— David Livingstone.

"No human being can describe the infinite; and what I saw was a part of infinity made visible and framed in beauty" — Edward Mohr.

AT THE VICTORIA FALLS the Zambezi, hitherto a somewhat placid river, suddenly kicks over the traces and plunges headlong into a sheer-sided chasm more than 100 metres deep and carved out of solid basalt rock.

For once the superlatives — magnificent, majestic, tumultuous, earthshattering — are justified. But the Victoria Falls are more than mere spectacle. They are an experience.

Though they had long been known to local people, who called them Mosi-oa-Tunya, or "The Smoke that Thunders", they were first revealed to the outside world by David Livingstone during the late 1850's.

Livingstone — who was a missionary first and explorer second — hoped to use the Zambezi as a navigable waterway, carrying trade goods between the coast and the interior. If he could open up such a route, he thought, the traffic in slaves which had plagued the peoples of the upper Zambezi for many years could be eradicated.

He failed in this overall objective — but he did succeed in publicising one of the most impressive natural wonders of the world.

The trickle of scientists and other explorers that followed him soon turned into a flood of traders, hunters, adventurers and even early tourists. By the turn of the century a considerable settlement had become established at the Falls. Some years later Imperial Airways inaugurated a flying-boat service, landing on the Zambezi a little way upstream where the old landing stage can still be seen. Today the Falls are easily accessible by road, rail and air and, together with the Hwange National Park, form one of Africa's finest tourist complexes.

One's impressions of the Falls depends very much on the time of year. During the dry season, the Zambezi's flow may dwindle to little more than a trickle. Parts of the Falls may dry out altogether. At these times the full extent of the width and depth of the gorges can be appreciated.

When the river is in flood, visibility can be restricted to a few metres by constant eruptions of drenching spray. But the sound, fury and raw power of a river, almost two kilometres wide, falling into a chasm 100 metres deep must be experienced to be understood.

Though most — like Livingstone and Mohr — are inspired to sometimes uncharacteristic flights of fancy by the Falls, others have adopted a different approach to the problem of doing them verbal justice. "It is hell itself" one early writer said, "a corner of which seems to open at your feet: a dark and terrible hell, from the middle of which you expect every moment to see some repulsive monster rising in anger."

But whatever their view, few remain unimpressed.

With a few exceptions, the Victoria Falls have avoided the excesses of development and "improvement" that have spoilt great scenic attractions the world over.

Today we can still see them much as did Thomas Baines, the artist who accompanied Livingstone on his journeys. Baines — apparently through no fault of his own — fell into disfavour with Livingstone and was later dismissed. But his painting have endured to show us how the Victoria Falls were first revealed to the rest of the world — and how little they have since been changed.

BUFFALO HUNT IN THE RAIN FOREST. THOMAS BAINES, 1863. © National Archives.

THE Falls have a fascinating geological history. They are not, as some early investigators believed, the result of some cataclysmic rending of the earth's crust. Instead, they have been created by the erosive power of the Zambezi itself as it cuts back through an immense block of basalt that was extruded as lava many millions of years ago, then buried under thick layers of sediment, and finally re-exposed in the relatively recent past.

The river has now cut through this basalt slab for almost a hundred kilometres, creating first of all the Batoka Gorge further downstream, and finally the falls themselves.

At least four separate sets of falls may have been formed and destroyed with the past ten thousand years. They are the result of transverse faults in the basalts, filled with softer rock. The Zambezi swiftly scoops out this softer material along the fault lines, so creating a waterfall that endures until the river finds a weak point in the lip, cuts back to the next fault, and then repeats the process.

Thus — although only a trained eye could detect any difference between the present-day Victoria Falls and those painted by Thomas Baines — they are in a state of constant geological change.

One day, no doubt, they will vanish altogether and the Zambezi will resume the kind of wandering course that it previously cut through the Batoka Gorge. We merely have the good fortune to live at a spectacular moment in geological history.

Upstream of the Victoria
Falls the river flows
peacefully past banks
lined with ilala palms, as
if totally oblivious of the
cataclysm to come.
The Zambezi has already
travelled many hundreds
of kilometres from its
source.
On its way it has
passed into Angola and
then through the

Barotseland floodplains, which trap the floodwaters of the rainy season and then release them slowly during May, June and July.
Here, just above the Falls, the flying boats once landed. Today, pleasure boats take visitors on relaxing sunset cruises, and anglers try to land the fierce-fighting tigerfish for which the Zambezi is famous.
Livingstone, once the capital of Zambia, lies close to the north bank. Most of the south bank, however, is included in the 57 500ha Zambezi National Park.
This gives visitors and tourists the opportunity to see many local animals at close quarters. The park contains large numbers of elephant and buffalo and a wide variety of antelopes such as eland, kudu, waterbuck and impala.

In the depths of the Batoka Gorge, below the Victoria Falls, the Zambezi is a different river altogether: nearly a hundred kilometres of waterfalls, thundering rapids, cataracts and white water confined between towering black cliffs.

Though Livingstone saw the gorge briefly on his way downstream, it was seldom visited until comparatively recently: it runs through terrain described by Frederick Selous as "among the roughest in the world."

And it is virtually impossible to walk along the bottom of the gorge, where huge chunks of basalt have tumbled from the cliffs and often present near-insuperable obstacles. The only way through is on the water.

First navigated early in the 1980's, Batoka is fast becoming a Mecca for whitewater rafters and canoists, who rank it among the most difficult stretches of river in the world.

Some wildlife manages to survive, even in these forbidding surroundings. Klipspringer live on the more gentle slopes; there are colonies of baboons and dassies among the rocks; and birds such as trumpeter hornbills call from the thin strip of riverine woodland above

the flood line.

Black eagle and fish eagle are also common, and the gorge is one of the few known breeding-grounds of the rare Taita falcon.

But its main attraction is its rugged scenery. There are many lesser waterfalls; long cataracts of roiling, green-and-white water; and sheer cliffs that vary in colour from pastel browns and russets, through purples, to jet black.

There are some surprises as well. Sometimes the tumult quietens for a while, and in such places the Zambezi has allowed miniature beaches of gleaming white sand to form. Behind them, rockpools lie hidden on the spacious flood platforms.

But overall the Batoka Gorge is threatening, even grimly sinister at times, its sides sheer and stark and its waters dangerous. The first Zimbabwean expedition to navigate the gorge was mounted by a local school, St George's College of Harare. It took the expedition almost two weeks to cover the 120km from the Victoria Falls to their destination a short way beyond the end of the gorge. Their rafts, manufactured from bamboo poles and tractor innertubes, broke up several times; capsizes were frequent; and injuries from hidden rocks were an ever-present hazard.

It is possible that the gorge may be dammed by a new hydroelectric scheme sometime before the turn of the century, to augment the power already provided by Lake Kariba and the Hwange schemes. Areas such as the lovely Moemba Falls, which lie roughly halfway down the gorge, will be lost. Livingstone, perhaps understandably after his experiences at the Victoria Falls, was not particularly impressed by Moemba or by the Batoka Gorge in general. Nevertheless, they are most attractive and deserve to be better known.

Unfortunately it is not easy for the casual visitor to see very much of the gorge. There is a path that leads down behind the Victoria Falls Hotel, and it is possible to visit Moemba using a four-wheel-drive vehicle. Otherwise, the only way to see the length of the gorge is to undertake one of the commercial rafting trips now available — and to drown the sound of pumping adrenalin in the roar of Batoka's gargantuan rapids.

The first accommodation at the Victoria Falls took the form of a shack built to house workers on what was at one time intended to become the Cape-to-Cairo railway link.

The magnificent Victoria Falls Hotel developed from these humble beginnings.

There is plenty to see and do, quite apart from enjoying the view of the Falls from the scenic vantage-points along their southern edge. Traditional dancers perform nightly at the hotels; curio shops offer examples of local craftsmanship.

Even though development at the Falls has by and large been moderate and unobtrusive, there are always dangers inherent in turning natural scenes into tourist attractions. At one time the rain forest, which lines the lip of the Falls, was in grave danger from the pressure of thousands of visitors.

And the unthinking may be tempted to pluck the rare plants and flowers that abound in the region. Protection of some kind is essential; and the Falls are today controlled by the Zimbabwean Department of National Parks, which has designated a few simple rules for visitors to ensure that the area remains unspoilt.

Recently the Falls gained one of the world's greatest conservation accolades: they were declared a World Heritage Site by UNESCO. This means that Zimbabwe has accepted the responsibility of protecting the Victoria Falls, not only on behalf of its own citizens, but on behalf of the world. Such an award is not made lightly: but, after spending a few days within sight and hearing of the Smoke that Thunders, few would doubt that they are worth the honour.

The
Hwange National Park

LOVE IT FOR ITS sunwashed immensity or hate it for its seemingly scorched monotony, one thing can be said for certain of Hwange: it is Zimbabwe's premier wildlife park, with some of the finest gatherings of wild animals to be seen in the whole of Africa.

Hwange — at over 12 000 sq.km. the biggest national park in the country — lies a short step from the Victoria Falls. It forms the north-eastern tip of the Kalahari desert — the immense, parched expanse of sand, scrub and occasional woodlands that reaches deep into the heart of neighbouring Botswana.

"Seemingly scorched monotony" because, although it is possible to drive through endless kilometres of apparently featureless bush, Hwange is really a symphony of subtle scenic variety and startling seasonal changes.

Broken country in the northwest of the park supports the mopane woodlands often characteristic of Zimbabwe's lower-lying areas. Further east, near the park headquarters at Main Camp, there are long forests of Zimbabwean teak. Near Hwange's south-eastern corner, strange "fossil dunes" roll across the landscape like long ocean swells. Only in the central and southern regions does the terrain

flatten out and extend for kilometre after kilometre of unrelieved sand and scrub — and even this wilderness has an attraction all of its own.

During the long dry season — and especially in September and October — Hwange does indeed present the appearance of an arid, scorched waste. But a short way below the surface there lie huge reserves of underground water which supply more than 60 artificial pans throughout the park.

And, in the rains, Hwange puts on a coat of brilliant emerald green and turns into a maze of tiny, ephemeral pans covered in waterlilies and fringed with reeds and sedges.

Hwange has never been inhabited by humans, except for occasional bands of wandering San bushmen who roamed the area many years ago.

Hwange has all Zimbabwe's indigenous animals in good numbers. It has some of Africa's biggest concentrations of elephant. There are big herds of buffalo; herds of eland, impala and sable; groups of zebra, waterbuck and kudu.

There is a multitude of smaller animals as well — jackals, bat-eared foxes, servals and civets, hares and mongooses.

And Hwange has more than 400 of Zimbabwe's 600-odd bird species and is an ornithologist's paradise.

Things were not always so. The area first become a wildlife reserve in the late 1920's, mainly because nobody could find any other use for it. At that time, uncontrolled hunting had reduced the region's elephant population to a mere 700.

Today Hwange has some 15 000 elephant, and both black and white rhinoceros have been reintroduced and are thriving. Careful management has created a park in which one is never far from wild

animals. Some of the
best sightings are to be
had close to Main Camp
and the Hwange Safari
Lodge, the hotel that
serves the park, at pans
such as Nyamandhlovu.

Other good viewing
areas are close to the
camps at Sinamatella and
Robins.

And it is one of
Zimbabwe's most easily
accessible parks as well.
There are air services
from Harare and the
Victoria Falls; and a good
tarred road leads directly
into the heart of the
park. Together with the
Victoria Falls, Hwange
forms one of the greatest
natural scenic and
wildlife complexes in
central Africa.

The great ease with which a casual visitor can see so wide a range of animals in Hwange is partly due to the manner in which the viewing tracks have been laid out.

These tracks give access to all the major pans at which wildlife tends to gather. But it is also due to the ecology of Hwange itself.

Because of the scarcity of surface water throughout much of the year, animals congregate in large numbers close to such water as is available.

Hence, during the dry months, it is an easy matter to position oneself at a much-frequented pan and to watch an apparently endless procession of animals as they come to the water, drink, and melt back into the bush.

But there is still an element of unpredictability that adds a sense of adventure and exploration to the experience. Some pans are often more favoured than others, and many of the artificially pumped pans hold saline water that seems to exert a particular attraction.

However, even these favoured pans may sometimes be deserted for a day or two. The animals simply seem to vanish into thin air. At such times patience and a little detective work are called for.

As well as the ubiquitous elephant, species such as buffalo, zebra, kudu, wildebeest, sable and impala are all regular visitors to the pans.

For those with limited time, Hwange is the finest park in Zimbabwe in which to see all these

species. Less predictable
— but still often sighted
during a stay of a few
days — are lion, leopard,
black and white rhinos,
roan antelopes, tsessebe
and even gemsbok in
some more remote
regions.

The best months
during which to see large
numbers of animals are
undoubtedly September
and October, when there
is no water except in the
pans. But a visit to
Hwange at any time of
year will bring its
rewards, even if animals
become a little harder to
find.

Few will have cause to
prompt the Hwange
ranger's retort to the
visitor who complained
that he had been in the
park all day and only
seen two tortoises.

"Two!" the ranger
replied. "You're lucky.
We usually only see
them in ones!"

Though some of Hwange's biggest concentrations of wildlife are often seen close to the park centres of Main Camp and the Sinamatella and Robins camps, it often pays to get off the beaten track a little.

In the west of the park, Mandavu Dam provides a chance to see animals not normally associated with Hwange: crocodiles and hippo.

In the east, the 100km drive that leads through the Makwa and Ngweshla pans, then south to the Kennedy series and ultimately back to Main Camp, passes through scenes that range from dense bush to the open grassy areas created by the "fossil rivers." These are the dried-out remnants of rivers which, in wetter times, once flowed south towards the Makgadigadi region in Botswana.

The track that goes further eastwards from Ngweshla Pan is usually only open to visitors staying with one of the commercial photosafari operators that use the park. But it gives access to several unusual areas. There are, for example, the grasslands at Mabisa, dotted with hundreds of stands of ilala palms. There are more grasslands at Ngamo, on Hwange's eastern tip. Ngamo is especially lovely during the rains, when thousands of wildebeest and giraffe can be found on wide plains that are more reminiscent of East Africa than of Zimbabwe. Ngamo also has one of the best concentrations of lion in Hwange.

The reasons for these strange changes in scenery are not fully known, but may have a lot to do with climatic changes in the relatively recent past.

The rolling fossil sand dunes indicate a drier period, when unbroken Kalahari sands may have blanketed the region; the fossilised riverlines, a wetter interlude.

It may take a little time to seek out this variety of scenes — but the visitor or wildlife photographer will find the result worth the effort.

An exhaustive list of Hwange's bird life is far beyond the scope of this book. Enough to say that the park holds more than 400 of Zimbabwe's 600-odd species.

Visitors should keep a good lookout for species such as the crowned cranes which, though not common elsewhere in the country, are often seen in several parts of the park.

Waterbirds such as knob-billed and white-faced duck and Egyptian geese often frequent the pans, and woolly-necked storks are a feature of the Ngamo grasslands at certain times of year. Most Zimbabwean raptors are present in good numbers; meanwhile the remains of kills made by predators such as lion or hyaena inevitably attract vultures and marabou storks.

Hwange is many things. But maybe most of all Hwange is a hundred elephants, stampeding to the water at the end of a long hot day; groups of cows with tiny calves at foot, browsing in the bush; and solitary bulls dozing beneath the trees.

Hwange now has the densest concentration of elephants in Africa, but the growth of this population — from 700 or so a few decades ago to more than 15 000 today — has brought its own problems.

Some of this growth has been attributable to protection under conservation laws. But the real problem is the confinement of elephants to a tiny fraction of their old ranges, when they could wander freely over many thousands of square kilometres.

The result was that the elephants began to destroy their own habitats. This has happened elsewhere in Africa: in Tsavo, Kenya, a once-thriving elephant population crashed to a few hundreds when it outstripped its food supply.

The managers of Hwange were faced with a grim decision: should the elephants be allowed to destroy the park's woodlands and grasslands — and maybe ultimately themselves? And should they be allowed to drive out all the smaller creatures that depend on the same sources of food?

Their answer was that a park is created to protect all its species — animals and plants — not merely the biggest and most spectacular. Elephant population control operations began in Hwange some years ago and have continued on and off ever since.

If elephant could be given more room in which to live: if their reproduction rates could adapt swiftly enough to cope with restrictions placed on them by human needs for land — then maybe the cull could be abandoned.

At least the policy means that Hwange has a good elephant population in some kind of balance with its environment. The alternative of destroyed habitat — and, soon after, no elephants either — is the worse of the twin evils.

What makes a man so love the wilderness? A great, flat, hot, arid, sandy, bushy stretch of wasteland such as Hwange? What magic — indefinable but so real — lures one back there time and time again? — T.V. Bulpin.

Lake Kariba

AFTER ITS tumultuous passage over the Victoria Falls and through the terrifying rapids of the Batoka Gorge, the Zambezi changes its character once again. It begins to slow: then comes to a virtual halt, as if exhausted by its recent turbulence, as it flows into the immense man-made lake of Kariba.

Few men can look upon great rivers without wishing to harness them to their use, and the Zambezi has been no exception. Usually it has resisted, and even the building of the Kariba dam was dogged by floods of an intensity never before recorded. But technology and engineering ultimately combined to harness the Zambezi to human benefit.

Big dams are not always good news. Their benefits — be they in the form of irrigation potential or hydroelectric power — can often be outweighed by the ecological damage they cause.

Nevertheless, Kariba is an established fact and arguments over its good or bad effects are largely academic. It seems to have escaped many of the problems often associated with big dams; and there is a timeless atmosphere about its blue waters and prolific wildlife that belies its mere 25 year history.

This atmosphere led one enthusiastic commentator to write, as he looked out over the lake and its shores, of "Africa unchanged, as it has been for centuries." Whatever else Kariba may be, it is certainly not "Africa unchanged." All the same, the comment was an undoubted tribute to the loveliness of Zimbabwe's inland sea.

KARIBA is 320km long, up to 30km wide, and when it was built it was the biggest man-made lake in the world. The wall was closed in 1958, and in 1960 the Queen Mother pressed the button that started the power flowing to the cities far to the south. By 1963 the dam was completely full and had submerged over 5 000sq.km. of bush, woodland and natural river.

It was designed with the sole purpose of providing hydroelectric power. Unlike many other large dams elsewhere in the world, it is not used for irrigation or water supplies.

Climate enforces certain constraints on the use of the Zambezi for hydroelectric power. Seasonal rains bring heavy floods for a month or two, followed by a long dry period during which the river's natural flow dwindles to a relative trickle. The dam's task is to trap the Zambezi floodwaters and to store them for use during the dry season. This, in effect, evens out the flow of the river and ensures a steady supply of water for the turbines throughout the year. Most of the water in Kariba comes, not from local rainfall, but from distant catchment areas in Zambia and Angola, on the Upper Zambezi. The floods may be delayed for several months by the meandering Barotseland floodplains. Thus the water level in the lake usually begins to rise in March, when the local rains have virtually ended.

It reaches its peak in July and then falls steadily for the rest of the year, when the outflow through the turbines is greater than the inflow from the Zambezi.

After a good rainy season excess water sometimes has to be "spilled" by opening the floodgates set high in the dam wall. It seldom happens that all six gates have to be opened simultaneously, but when they are, the resulting maelstrom is one of Zimbabwe's most impressive sights.

Sometimes the problem is too little water, not too much. During the early 1980's, when most of southern Africa was hit by drought, the level of water in Kariba fell some ten metres below the normal high-water mark. Zimbabwe is a landlocked country; the lake created an immense playground and has become one of the country's greatest tourist attractions.

It has also been developed as a fishery. A commercial netting industry harvests and sells bream and other species. Meanwhile, the so-called "kapenta" — a freshwater sardine — was introduced into Kariba in the late 1960's. It has created a new industry that provides large quantities of cheap protein for local and foreign markets.

And easy access to wildlife is another benefit brought by Kariba. The Matusadona National Park, a short way across the lake from the town and dam wall, gives visitors the chance to see animals such as elephant, buffalo, hippo and impala from the safety of specially-built viewing craft.

The dam wall itself, which contains more than a million cubic metres of concrete, was built by an Italian consortium.

But before work could begin, the problem of access to the site had to be overcome. Kariba lay in the midst of remote, rugged country that suffered from extremes

of heat, malarial mosquitoes, and all the other discomforts of the Zambezi Valley.

At first it was thought that the road to Kariba would take enormous amounts of money and time to build. But then someone had a brainwave: follow the elephants.

The road from Makuti to Kariba was finally built, at a fraction of the original cost, along age-old elephant trails.

Preliminary work began. But there was another, much bigger problem: the 57,000 BaTonga people who lived in the Gwembe Valley, as the region upstream of the dam site used to be called. All would have to be moved out and relocated elsewhere before the dam began to fill.

Many BaTongas believed that the talk of a dam was merely a scheme to evict them from these lands. Others refused to believe that an event such as the flooding of the entire region could ever take place. Nyaminyami, their rivergod, they said, would never permit such

a monstrous tampering with the great river.

And they were very nearly right. In 1957, soon after building had begun, a flood of unprecedented intensity swept down the Zambezi. A flood of this size, it was thought, could be expected only once in every thousand years. After a massive cleanup operation, however, building recommenced.

But during the following year's rains, in 1958, an even bigger flood arrived. This time the cofferdams were overtopped, the

footbridge swept away, and the work already done came close to destruction. Had this happened, the entire future of the dam would have been jeopardised — and Nyaminyami would have won.

He didn't; but it was a close thing. This flood

was christened the "one-in-ten-thousand-year" flood. The engineers designed two more floodgates into the wall and, once again building was restarted.

After that Nyaminyami seems to have given up. The dam was completed and the turbines started.

Finally the Italians left. They also had their tragedies: several workers were killed during the building of the dam. They are commemorated in the charming little church on the Kariba heights.

And Nyaminyami? You can buy his effigy today for a few dollars in the shops and hotels around the lake. An apparently harmless little curiosity — but he almost halted the building of the biggest man-made lake in the world. and the BaTongas are still not altogether certain that he has finished with Kariba.

Today Kariba has become one of the biggest tourist centres in Zimbabwe. Hotels and bushcamps dotted along the lake shore provide a variety of diversions: sailing, boating, waterskiing, fishing and wildlife viewing tours. Luxurious cruise-boats travel up and down the lake or wander among its islands, bays and estuaries.

Many visitors travel little further than the hotels and casinos of Kariba itself, and miss much of what the lake can offer. Away from the town and the dam wall the shores are often deserted, and given over to wildlife in parks such as the Matusadona, on the southern shore a short boat ride from Kariba.

There are still plenty of reminders that, in natural terms, Kariba has only just been born. Many of the shores are still lined with the skeletons of the trees that died as the waters rose. In places they form vast forests of strangely weird beauty.

They also conceal shorelines composed of hundreds of tiny creeks and inlets populated with hippo, crocodiles and a plethora of bird life.

In such creeks can be seen the huge Goliath herons, tiny malachite kingfishers, storks, and of course fish eagles — the birds that, above all others, symbolise the Zambezi and Kariba.

Kariba probably has one of the biggest fisheagle populations in Africa. Strongly territorial birds, they mate for life and delight in building their untidy nests in the bare branches of the dead trees.

Many of the shores have been colonised by a grass, which used to occupy swampy areas on the natural Zambezi. It has spread to form immense swards that develop as the lake falls during the dry season. In this way it creates a vast reserve of food for elephant, impala, hippo, and for the buffalo herds up to 1 000-strong that often roam the lake shore.

The best way to explore such areas is on a small boat that can slip in and out of the trees and into the shallowest of inlets. And a boat gives access to many of Kariba's other attractions as well.

There is, for example, the majestic Sanyati Gorge on the western edge of the Matusadona National Park. A former Zambezi tributary, it now forms a fiord that extends more than ten kilometres inland and provides some of the finest tigerfishing on the lake.

In the Sanyati, too, the more fortunate may spot leopard sunning themselves on the rocks.

Further west lie the Ume, Sengwa and Ruzihururu rivers, more

gentle in character. Finally, more than 300km west of the dam wall, the lake begins to narrow and then ends in the depths of the Devils Gorge.

On the one hand Kariba has consistently provided cheap electricity to Zimbabwe and Zambia for more than a quarter of a century. This, in turn, has been of immense value in the development of local industry.

It provides a huge holiday playground for local and overseas visitors, and creates many opportunities for sport and recreation.

On the other hand, Kariba destroyed a great amount of land and forest in a region that needs ever-increasing amounts of these valuable commodities, and its ultimate ecological effects may not be known for many years.

Maybe it is best simply to look at Kariba as yet another fascinating aspect of the Zambezi: one that has been harnessed by man for his own use, maybe, but that has acquired an attraction and a beauty of its own.

But what was the Zambezi like before the dam was built? To see the river in its natural state we have travel further downstream, beyond the dam wall, to the great wilderness of Mana Pools and the Middle Zambezi Valley.

The
Middle Zambezi
Valley

AT THE END of the Kariba gorge, a few kilometres downstream of the dam wall, the hills gradually fall back on either side of the Zambezi. The river broadens and slows, and begins to split into a maze of channels running between grass-topped islands and glistening sandbanks populated by hippo and crocodiles.

This is the Middle Zambezi Valley, created by the same process that formed the spectacular rift system of East Africa. It takes the shape of a wide, almost flat valley floor, covered in dense bush and woodland, and shut away from the outside world by the steep escarpments that run up to 50km distant from the river. The Valley, a 10 000sq.km. wilderness, has become one of the finest wildlife areas in southern Africa. It holds more than 12 000 elephant; maybe 30 000 buffalo; and it has the best remaining population of the rare black rhinoceros in the world.

Unlike Lake Kariba or the Victoria Falls, the Zambezi Valley has not been intensively developed for tourism. There are a couple of commercial bushcamps on the river, but by and large the emphasis is on solitude and self-sufficiency. In the heart of the Valley lies the Mana Pools National Park, widely regarded as the loveliest park in Zimbabwe. Across the river, the Zambian escarpment rises in tiers of bush-clad hills. At one's back, long woodlands of acacias and mahoganies stretch along the banks of the Zambezi for many kilometres. And in between runs the Middle Zambezi at its most beautiful — unharnessed, untamed and entirely natural.

The heart of the Middle Zambezi Valley lies at Mana Pools, where thousands of elephant, buffalo, zebra, kudu, eland, impala and baboons gather close to the Zambezi during the dry season.

In the Mana Pools area the Zambezi has slowly wandered northwards across the Valley floor over the past few millennia. Long-abandoned river channels now harbour secret little pools lined with ebonies and figs. Meanwhile woodlands of acacias, mahoganies, leadwoods and raintrees have grown on the fertile soils left behind by the retreating river.

Mana's plentiful wildlife undertakes a slow, regular seasonal movement to and from the Zambezi. During the rains, almost all the large animals desert the river and vanish into the immense Zambezi Valley hinterland.

For most of the year this hinterland is harsh and inhospitable. During the rains, however, the pans fill briefly, and there is a flush of fresh grazing and new leaf. The animals stay here, often far distant from the Zambezi, as long as food and water are easily available.

Soon after the rains end, though, the wildlife is forced back towards the Zambezi by shortages of food and water in the hinterland. At Mana Pools, and for many kilometres along the river on either side, they find an enormous reserve of grazing and browsing. The acacias, in particular, are beloved of the elephant. These trees are unusual: they lose their leaves in the rains, and come into leaf in the dry season. Elephant reach up and pluck twigs and branches from the trees, or shake the trunks to bring down the succulent pods they bear in August and September.

Mana and the Zambezi support thousands of animals through the worst of the dry season. There are impala and baboon everywhere. Herds of kudu, zebra and eland wander through the woodlands and drink from the river or the pools; buffalo congregate in herds up to 2 000-strong.

The focal point of all this activity is, of course, the Zambezi itself. It creates a plentiful, year-round supply of water in the parched heart of the Zambezi Valley. It supports some of Zimbabwe's best populations of hippo and crocodiles. And, of course, the bird life is magnificent — fisheagles, herons, kingfishers, plovers, waders and, a particular feature, several colonies of the beautiful carmine bee-eaters.
This is really the wildest part of a wild river. The Middle Zambezi Valley wilderness was barely known until well into this century. And even today some areas, such as the Chewore mountains, downstream of Mana Pools, are seldom visited.

Since they were opened up to visitors, the Zambezi Valley and the Mana Pools National Park have become firm favourites with discerning wildlife people from Zimbabwe and abroad. Though many stay at the national parks camps strung along the riverbank, a couple of commercial operations provide facilities for those who prefer their wilderness to be tempered with a little comfort.

However, one of Mana's greatest attractions is the manner in wich visitors can walk, alone and unaccompanied, through some of the finest wildlife country in Zimbabwe.

This is a rare privilege. In most parks, visitors are confined to their vehicles or to designated picnic sites. This inevitably creates something of a barrier between them and the beauty they have come to experience.

On foot, however, the barriers are down. We are able to return, alone and unaided, to the wilderness in which we were born, millions of years ago.

This is a frightening prospect to many. In fact it is probably less dangerous than crossing a busy city street. The dangers of unprovoked attacks from wild animals are generally small — and the observance of a few simple rules can virtually eliminate them altogether.

And Mana offers some superb walking, especially among the park-like acacias and mahoganies that flank the river in many places. Others prefer to canoe down the Zambezi and this, too, is a superb experience, traversing the entire range of scenery the river and the valley can offer.

Such a voyage might begin at the Kariba dam wall, or further downstream. Aided by a current that takes most of the effort out of the exercise, the traveller soon finds himself among the sandbanks and islands of Mana Pools, where crocodiles and schools of hippo add spice to the experience. He may then linger in the hyacinth-lined channels that lie in the Sapi Safari Area, downstream of Mana Pools, before plunging into the 30km Mupata Gorge.

Once through Mupata, it is a short distance to Kanyemba, the tiny outpost at the eastern end of the Middle Zambezi Valley. Here the river slows again as it enters another man-made lake, that of Cabora Bassa in Mocambique. And here, too, ends the natural Middle Zambezi — one more face of the river that has already passed through the turmoil of the Victoria Falls and Batoka Gorge and the peace and tranquillity of Lake Kariba.

The Harare Region

SCENES FROM HARARE, the Zimbabwean capital, were flashed into millions of homes throughout the world when the country achieved its independence in 1980.

But perhaps it is only the air traveller who sees the city in its true perspective: a tiny enclave of modern buildings, ringed by vast suburbs beyond which there stretches the immensity of bush and farmland so typical of the Zimbabwean highveld.

Most of the world's older cities grew over the centuries from small beginnings — usually beside natural harbours, at the crossroads of great trade routes, or on top of natural reserves of minerals or other resources.

Harare did none of these things. It was arbitrarily sited, in the midst of what was then sparsely-inhabited bush, in the 1890's by the first settlers to make a determined effort to colonise the country.

The original settlement was at the foot of the Kopje, the small hill that forms so striking a landmark amid its otherwise generally flat surroundings. However, the main development soon began to take place a short distance to the north east.

The city's regular grid pattern of streets and avenues was planned in the 1890's, beginning with First Street.

Photographs taken at the time show striking contrasts: brand-new buildings in stone and brick rose from featureless grasslands, in splendid isolation, sometimes still flanked by the pole-and-daga huts of the original settlers.

During the present century a road system hesitantly fanned out from the new city and gave access to Bulawayo

and the Midlands, the south and south-east, and later to Kariba and Lusaka. A railway, built at great cost in both lives and money, was driven through harsh country from the Indian Ocean coast at Beira; and another rail link was forged with Bulawayo.

Meanwhile the city's airport grew from small beginnings until, at one time, it boasted the longest runway in the world. This was rendered necessary by Harare's altitude and temperatures. At 1 471 metres above sea level, the city is effectively perched on a mountain top disguised by the

gentle slopes of the Zimbabwean plateau. And, although it enjoys one of the most agreeable climates in Africa, with long hours of sunshine and wet weather generally confined between the months of November and March, summer temperatures can climb into the 40's.

The city slowly expanded and developed until today it accommodates the best part of a million inhabitants; and during the past two decades its skyline was dramatically altered by the advent of the high-rise buildings clustered in the city centre.

Largely as a result of its early history, the city tends to cluster round two distinct centres. One lies near the foot of the Kopje, in the teeming area around Pioneer Street and Charter Road. Here can be found multitudes of smaller shops and the bustling atmosphere of the market place. The other centre, in the shopping areas of First Street and its environs, is more luxuriantly expensive, more sedate — and, according to many, considerably less interesting.

Harare is surrounded by suburbs, some of which — such as Chitungwiza — have developed into satellite towns in their own right. The pattern was again set early in the city's history: luxurious houses on large plots to the north, cheaper houses to the south and west — and the so-called "high density" suburbs, in huge clusters often far distant from the city centre.

First impressions of Harare are striking enough. The city centre has a park-like atmosphere, with broad streets lined with jacarandas, flamboyants, and spathodias. There are spacious gardens; excellent restaurants; and all the usual tourist "sights" such as museums, art galleries and municipal and Parliament buildings.

These things are easy enough to locate with the help of a tourist guidebook. However, finding the true soul of

the city is less easy. It functions primarily as a manufacturing and service centre for the rest of the country; and most of all it probably lies in the high density suburbs and in the industrial areas flanking the city — seldom visited by the average tourist.

Every day an immense tidal wave of workers flows from these suburbs to the industrial areas. Motor vehicles, locomotives and rolling stock, furniture, glass, clothing, food and drink, agricultural, irrigation and mining equipment are all made in Harare; and a great number of smaller companies provide supporting services and expertise.

More conventionally, though, the visitor has access to Harare's several parks and its nine public swimming pools, and to its Civic Centre with its library, museum, music college and concert hall. Several theatres and cinemas provide a year-round series of productions for all tastes. Educational institutions include the University of Zimbabwe, the Harare Polytechnic, Gwebi Agricultural College and many primary and secondary schools.

And those wishing to acquire an all-round knowledge of Zimbabwe and its people would do well to visit the National Archives, the Queen Victoria Museum and the National Gallery.

It was the siren lure of another "El Dorado" that was largely responsible for early interest in the region that is now Mashonaland. Spurred on by tales of ancient gold workings, many new settlers based their dreams of wealth on the possibility of finding new gold-bearing reefs comparable to that of the Rand.

In this they were disappointed. The region's total output up to 1898 was valued at £8 050 — a poor return on hundreds of thousands of pounds invested.

Nonetheless, gold eventually became Zimbabwe's most valuable export until 1946, when it was overtaken by tobacco.

Every city has a unique feature all of its own, and in Harare this place is undoubtedly occupied by the annual tobacco auctions.

Tobacco finally came to be the "gold" upon which much of Zimbabwe's fortune has been based, and this commodity has been the country's foremost export earner for more than three decades.

Each year more than 1 000 growers produce over 100 000 tonnes of tobacco of various types and grades. Over 90% is sold abroad, making Zimbabwe one of the major exporting nations in the world and probably around fourth in terms of actual production.

To sell this crop, a massive and extremely efficient auctioning system has been developed, and the Harare auction floors are the largest in the world. during which there is a steady flow of tobacco bales from the agricultural areas around Harare to the auction floors. Thus the auctions go on while reaping continues.

When they reach the floors, the bales are registered and weighed before being transported to the auction floors on trolley trains. The auction system itself demands a high level of skill, endurance and concentration from the selling team.

The auctions get under way with the team on one side of a long line of bales: the starter, who calls the farmer's starting price; the auctioneer himself; and two ticket writers who mark the buyer's number and price on each bale as it is sold.

On the other side of the line of bales are the buyers, who make their bids with a nod or a lifted finger.

The entire crop is not reaped at once. As leaves ripen from the bottom of the plant they are stripped, cured and graded. The season lasts for over five months,

Harare is also the headquarters of the Zimbabwe Broadcasting Corporation, the country's national radio and television service.

Covering all urban centres and a growing proportion of rural areas, the ZBC has four radio stations and a television service and employs more than 600 people.

Since Independence the corporation has undergone a period of overhaul and expansion, including the introduction of new equipment and the

necessary technical training of new young members of staff.

Most of the corporation's radio and television programmes are compiled at studios in Harare and then beamed to Bulawayo, where they are rebroadcast after local content has been added as required.

The country's most popular radio station — and its first fully-fledged commercial station — is Radio Three. From its early-morning opening to its midnight closedown, Radio Three offers a continuous menu of lively, upbeat programmes.

Radio One is in a rather quieter vein, often leaning towards classical music and serious drama, mainly in English, while Radio Two offers a similar mix but predominantly in the two local languages of Shona and Ndebele.

Maybe the most interesting and exciting development in recent years has been the inauguration of Radio Four, a primarily eductional medium that commenced broadcasting in October 1982. Radio Four collaborates closely with the Ministry of Education for whom, during school terms, it broadcasts more than three hours of daily programmes aimed at children.

Meanwhile, a short distance from the corporation's Borrowdale radio headquarters, the nation's television service has been re-equipped virtually from to to bottom with up-to-date equipment.

Though unique, Shona sculpture shares features with art from other African cultures.

Themes and symbols from centuries of heritage and tradition are expressed in tangible form and often reflect the deeprooted consciousness of good and evil that the sculptors experience in the world around them.

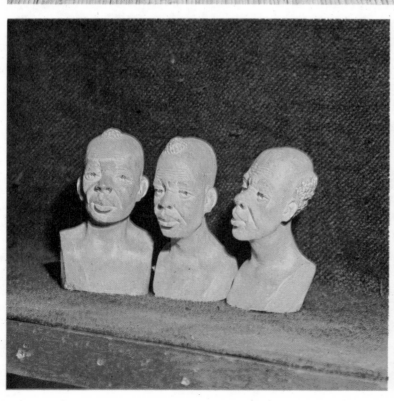

The Zimbabwean highveld in the region of Harare is mainly given over to commercial farmlands that produce cattle, maize, tobacco, wheat and a wide variety of other crops.

Those in search of the great expanses of wilderness and plentiful wildlife populations for which Zimbabwe is reknowned will have to travel further — to such areas as Hwange, Kariba or the Zambezi Valley.

Nevertheless, the Harare region provides opportunities for many kinds of recreation, from the pursuit of sporting activities to the study of local flora and fauna in the botanical gardens and nature reserves to be found in and around the city.

Within the city limits there are the Mukuvisi Woodlands, an area of natural highveld woodland untouched by development and recently turned into a conservation and environmental education centre.

The Mukuvisi Woodlands are managed by an association consisting of representatives from several leading conservation societies, and will eventually provide educational facilities for 100 000 schoolchildren each year.

Further out of town, on the Bulawayo road, lies the longer-established McIlwaine Recreational Park. Based on the dam

that supplies Harare with much of its drinking water, McIlwaine is controlled and run by the Zimbabwe Department of National Parks and Wild Life Management.

Its aim is to provide opportunities for recreation and nature studies to Harare residents, and the park offers comfortable accommodation in well-equipped chalets and lodges as well as camping and caravanning facilities.

The north bank is the base for a variety of recreational activities, notably boating, fishing and sailing. Zimbabwe has a strong and keen dinghy racing fraternity and races take place on the lake over most weekends.

In contrast, the south bank has been set aside as a wildlife reserve with good populations of many local animals. Sable, wildebeast, impala, waterbuck and kudu feature prominently, and there is a good and easily visible population of the less common tsessebe.

In common with Lake Kyle, the Matopos and other smaller Zimbabwean parks, McIlwaine has its own group of the rare white rhinoceros, the second largest living land mammal.

As is the case elsewhere, the McIlwaine rhinos have developed from stock first brought in from Natal, where the

species was rescued from extinction during the 1980's in one of this century's greatest conservation success stories.

Visitors can also see crocodiles at close quarters in the holding pens beside the lake, and the Department of National Parks also maintains its own research facility within the park.

On the other side of town, on the Shamva road, lies an attraction of an altogether different nature: the Ewanrigg Botanical Gardens, which forms one of the finest collections of indigenous and exotic plants in southern Africa.

Ewanrigg is especially noteworthy for its magnificent display of aloes, which come into bloom during the winter months of June and July, and is, like McIlwaine, controlled and maintained by the Department of National Parks. It also features a new and extensive herb garden.

The more venturesome may first travel out to the famous Chinhoyi Caves, formed within the limestone hills of the area, and might then continue on to the strange Palm Block, which lies in the midst of magnificent country towards the Zambezi escarpment. These reserves contain Zimbabwe's only specimens of the huge raphia palm.

The Bulawayo Region

BULAWAYO lies in the midst of the vast, often flat, yet immensely attractive surroundings of Matabeleland, the focal point of much of Zimbabwe's romance and early history.

The region provides evidence of some of Zimbabwe's earliest human inhabitants: the Stone Age "bushmen." They occupied the caves in the Matobo Hills, which lie south of the city and form one of the country's finest scenic areas. The Stone Age paintings are the legacy of a culture which, though beset by all the problems inherent in its hunter-gatherer way of life, yet had the time to create some of the most beautiful primitive works of art in the world.

Much later in history, the Shona stonebuilding culture, which constructed the huge and mysterious Great Zimbabwe near Masvingo, spread into Matabeleland. They have left us the intricate stonework of the ruins at Khami, Naletale and Dhlodhlo.

During the 19th century, when the first outside settlers had begun to filter into the region, Bulawayo had already become the royal capital first of Mzilikazi and then of Lobengula, the early Ndebele kings.

After that, a long and proud history was overtaken by the growth of a modern city in the heart of the Matabeleland bush. Bulawayo became a railway town; then a booming industrial centre; and much of the surrounding bush was turned over to cattle ranching. Today, Bulawayo is Zimbabwe's second city and has regular rail and air links with major centres both inside and outside Zimbabwe.

With a population of more than 400 000, Bulawayo is Zimbabwe's second largest city. It is the site of the country's main railway junction and lies roughly halfway between Beitbridge and the Victoria Falls.
The area now occupied by the modern city had long been a major centre for the Ndebele people when it was taken over by settlers in 1893. Though the new city began to expand almost immediately, the beginnings of a boom were abruptly stifled when the settlers were forced to defend themselves against a spirited attempt by the Ndebeles to eject them in 1896.
This was, in effect, one of the earliest

manifestations of the liberation wars that were to follow. However, though not defeated, the Ndebeles were persuaded to accept the new culture in their midst and Bulawayo began to expand again. The impressive buildings of Zimbabwe's National Museum are located in Centenary Park. Mainly concerned with natural history, the museum is among the finest institutions of its kind in southern Africa.

Its mammal collection, with 75 000 specimens, is the largest in the southern hemisphere and the eighth largest in the world.

The National Railways of Zimbabwe have their headquarters in the city, together with a fascinating museum that includes locomotives, rolling stock and exhibits of machinery dating back beyond the turn of the century. Of especial interest are the antique locomotives and the "museum on wheels" — a 1904 passenger coach restored to its original fittings and livery.

Though much of the country has now been electrified, Zimbabwe is still something of a Mecca for railway enthusiasts because of the numbers of steam locomotives still running.

Recreational areas around the city include the Hillside, Ncema, Umzingwane and Khami dams. The city also has an educational nature reserve on its doorstep at Tchabalala, on the road to the Matobo Hills.

However, Bulawayo is solidly based on its industry. Some 600 factories produce an immense array of products. The city has the biggest concentration of heavy and light engineering concerns in Zimbabwe. There are many textile and clothing factories, and one of the

country's principal electronics manufacturing centres. Agriculturally, Bulawayo is the hub of a substantial ranching industry spread throughout Matabeleland, and the mines in the region produce nearly half Zimbabwe's output. From them come asbestos, chrome, copper, coal, gold, mica, tin, nickel and emeralds, and a growing volume of semi-precious stones.

The Cyrene Mission church, which lies a little more than 30km from the Bulawayo city centre, boasts some of the loveliest examples of inspirational art in Zimbabwe.

Cyrene was established as a primary boarding school in 1939, and taught art as one of its major subjects right from its earliest days.

The interior of the church is dominated by the magnificent paintings on its eastern wall, behind the altar. The large figures, from left to right, include Mquamesela, the first Zulu martyr; Bernard Mizeke, the first Shona martyr; the Living Christ; Simon of Cyrene, carrying the cross; and Masomela, the girl martyr of Sukukuniland.

The legend around the figure of Christ is in Sindebele, as is the wording on the rest of the paintings. It reads — "by this shall all men know you are my disciples — if you love one another."

The complete wall opposite the altar is devoted to a fresco of the Last Judgment. Its general theme is that of artists, craftsmen and workers "lifting up" their work to Christian judgment.

Meanwhile, an exterior wall of the church is used as the "canvas" for a portrayal of the Crucifixion, carved from old railway sleepers.

Another unique Zimbabwean institution, the Chipangali Wildlife Orphanage, also lies a few kilometres from the Bulawayo city centre. The orphanage cares for wild animals and birds that have been injured or orphaned, and was founded in the early 1970's.

Many animals come to Chipangali after being involved in road accidents. Birds, such as flamingoes, are often injured in collisions with power lines. They are treated, kept in spacious enclosures, and released back into the wild whenever possible. But many other animals arrive at Chipangali after they have been rejected by people who have tried to rear them as pets. In a country like Zimbabwe it is all too easy to obtain young animals of all kinds, from mongooses to lion and leopard.

During its history Chipangali has created some of the finest captive collections of rare animals in the world. The orphanage has one of a handful of packs of wild dog ever to be reared in captivity. It has breeding groups of the uncommon brown hyaena, and of the beautiful serval cats. Research now forms an important part of Chipangali's activities, as it provides unique opportunities to study living specimens of many species that are almost

impossible to research successfully in the wild. Besides large cats such as lion, leopard, serval and caracal, the orphanage has many antelopes and numerous birds including flamingoes, raptors and waterfowl. Chipangali is open to the public and indeed depends on the generosity of visitors and donors for its survival.

THE Khami, Naletale and Dhlodhlo ruins, all of which are located in the Bulawayo region, bear witness to the spread of stoneworking peoples from their main centre at the Great Zimbabwe. The Shona culture that built them first became established at the Great Zimbabwe and flourished between the 13th and 15th centuries. At some point these people spread across much of Zimbabwe, bringing their stoneworking abilities with them.

Meanwhile the fascinating Matobo Hills, south of Bulawayo, contain plenty of evidence of a far older culture: that of the Stone Age people who occupied the natural rock caves and shelters in the hills up to 40 000 years ago.

The Matobo Hills are one of the most mysteriously attractive of all Zimbabwean wild places, with an atmosphere that varies from innocuously

spectacular during a spring afternoon to broodingly mysterious under a rising moon. The hills have been almost continuously occupied by humans for the last 40 000 years, except for the glacial periods of the Ice Ages. Evidence for this occupation comes both from the rock paintings, and from the successive layers of human refuse excavated from the floors of caves and shelters

such as Nswatugi, on the road to the fenced Whovi wildlife area, and Pomongwe Cave, a couple of kilometres from the National Parks headquarters at Maleme Dam.

Both contain plentiful examples of rock art, and the paintings at Nswatugi are among the finest of their kind in the world. The artists were hunter-gatherers, and depended for their survival on whatever they could hunt or glean from their environment. The most commonly depicted subjects, apart from human, are antelopes and larger mammals, and this can tell us something of the wildlife indigenous to the hills.

Kudu and giraffe are often painted, buffalo less so; but this may merely be an indication of aesthetic preference. However, it was the unmistakeable portrayal of white rhino in a rock shelter in the hills that encouraged the Department of National Parks to restock the area with these animals.

Today, white rhino are a common sight within the part of the Matobo Hills managed by the Department.

Besides scenery and Stone Age art, the hills now offer sightings of many local wildlife species. Most have been reintroduced into the area after human populations were moved out earlier in the century

in order to protect its sensitive watersheds, springs, and seeps. Several species are of particular interest. One is the leopard: these beautiful animals, though seldom seen by daytime visitors, are common throughout the hills, which provide a perfect habitat for this nocturnal hunter. Prey species such as baboons and dassies are abundant, although studies in the hills have shown that leopard may eat almost anything from antelopes to scorpions. Over 50 percent of all Zimbabwean bird species have been recorded in the hills, including 40 species of raptor and more than 100 black eagle nests.

Great Zimbabwe, Lake Kyle, and the South East Lowveld

SOUTH EASTERN ZIMBABWE presents us with a strange mix of ancient history and legend, modern agriculture, and remote, undeveloped wilderness.

Its focal point lies at the Great Zimbabwe, the amazing stone structure that lies a little way from the small town of Masvingo.

Even today the controversy sometimes crops up: were Zimbabwe's goldbearing lands the site of the biblical Ophir? And did they provide the riches of the courts of Solomon, Sheba and Hiram?

Though we may never know the answer to this particular question, one thing is certain: the region was a centre of trade with Arab peoples for many centuries prior to recorded history.

In the circumstances, then, the early explorers may perhaps be forgiven for assuming that the Great Zimbabwe was originally built by these ancient traders. The truth, of course, is that it was built by local Shona peoples.

South of Masvingo and the Great Zimbabwe lie both Zimbabwe's most ambitious irrigation project, carved out of virgin bush, and some of the country's most remote wilderness in the Gonarezhou National Park.

Here, too, legends abound. There are said to be old Arab mooring rings buried in the sands of the Save-Lunde confluence; and there are tales of "lost cities" hidden in the depths of the bush.

Neither may be true. But the stories add a patina of mystery to a region already made fascinating enough by the mere presence of Great Zimbabwe alone.

GREAT Zimbabwe, near Masvingo, covers an area of 720 hectares and is the site of the most spectacular remains of human building in Africa south of the Sahara.

This vast complex of ruined enclosures and walls is all that is left of a city that once spread over several square

kilometres and housed a population of some 10 000 people.

Rumours of the existence of the ruins had often trickled through to Portuguese traders on the coast. But, so far as the outside world was concerned, the first genuine eyewitness description of the ruins was provided by the German explorer, Karl Mauch, in the 1870's.

During its heyday the Zimbabwe was the prestigious capital city of a thriving state that gradually spread its culture over much of the Zimbabwean highveld.

But the wealthy state eventually began to decline during the later 15th century. The immediate cause of the collapse was probably ecological. The deserted city fell into disuse, then decay. But the extent of the ruins still standing bears eloquent testimony to the skills of their original builders.

THE location of Zimbabwe was probably determined by the unusually moderate climate of the area, which makes it an island of green among the more usual browns and greys of the winter months.

The rocks in the surrounding hills were suitable for building, and indeed the hill complex, sometimes called the "acropolis", is sited on a sheer granite cliff almost 100 metres high.

This may have been the king's dwelling place. Smaller enclosures along the ridge include the so-called Smelting Enclosure, the Ironstone Cave, and the Ritual Enclosure, where many of the famous soapstone Zimbabwe Birds were found.

The Great Enclosure, which lies in the valley at the southern foot of the hill, is the largest, best preserved — and probably the most photographed — of all the remains. Built some time after the hill complex, it is more or less elliptical in shape and is 106 metres across at its widest. The massive outer wall stands 11 metres high and is more than 243 metres in circumference. The enclosure contains roughly 18 000 cubic metres of stonework of a very high order, which makes it the biggest single ancient structure in sub-Saharan Africa.

This may have been the court and dwelling-place of the king's wives. Within the enclosure there also stands the enigmatic conical tower, a solid stone structure that contains some of the finest architecture and stonework of all.

Eleven metres high, with a diameter at it s base of almost six metres, the tower has long puzzled archaeologists.

Stretching across the rest of the valley are the remains of hundreds of dry stone enclosures. Many valuable relics and artefacts have been

found here, where it is believed that the lesser dignitaries of the king's court may have been housed.

It is difficult, today, to picture what once might have been here. The ruins we see today would have been surrounded by the pole-and-daga huts of the ordinary citizens. Even within the stone enclosures themselves, the occupants will have lived in similar huts.

We can picture Great Zimbabwe, much like a modern city, slowly growing and becoming ever more sophisticated — until the lands become overgrazed and bare, the hills denuded of their trees, and the stonework gradually becoming shabby and falling into disrepair.

And finally — desertion, except for a few stragglers living in the ruins of former glories. Trees began to sprout among the stones, the grass to grow among the enclosures: and, over it all — silence, except for the sighing of the wind through the crumbling walls.

Today, of course, Great Zimbabwe has been preserved and tidied, as befits the nation's greatest symbol of its past. Even so, when we stand among the deserted walls, we can give play to the imagination: is that the chatter of some fellow-visitors — or of the king's wives?

Lake Kyle is Zimbabwe's second biggest dam after Lake Kariba and was built on the Mtilikwe river as part of an immense water storage system to feed the irrigation schemes in the south-east lowveld.

The lake extends over 90sq.km. and features one of the most varied shorelines of any of Zimbabwe's inland waters, ranging from granite cliffs to rocky beaches lined with trees.

Kyle has become popular with sailing and boating enthusiasts, and also provides the best black bass fishing in the country. A yearly international competition attracts anglers from all over Africa.

The lake is also the focal point of a so-called "recreational park", situated on its northern shore. Recreational parks, which have a lower conservation status than the fullscale National Parks, are often created around artificial lakes such as Kyle.

Within the Kyle recreational park more than 60km of winding roads enable visitors to see a wide variety of antelopes. Some, such as the oribi, Lichtenstein's hartebeest and nyala, are seldom seen in other

parks.

The area also contains buffalo, giraffe, and several groups of the rare white rhinoceros.

These gentle creatures — the second largest living land mammals in the world — have a dramatic history. They came close to total extinction throughout southern Africa earlier this century because of uncontrolled hunting.

However, a tiny relict population was given intensive protection in Natal, and this nucleus eventually bred until it numbered over a thousand animals.

At this point it became possible to start relocating groups of white rhinos into areas where they had formerly lived.

The white rhino takes its name from the Afrikaans word meaning "wide", and which refers to the animal's mouth.

South east of Masvingo, Kyle and the Great Zimbabwe, the Zimbabwean plateau falls away towards the immense, hot and formerly remote expanse known generally as the lowveld, or low country.

A few decades ago the entire region was covered by virgin bush occupied only by a few scattered peoples, thousands of wild animals, and one or two cattle ranches in areas clear of the tsetse fly.

In many parts of the lowveld the animals are still there, especially in the Gonarezhou National Park on the Mozambique border and in the neighbouring wildlife ranches.

But a 200,000ha expanse of former bush now produces crops such as sugarcane and cotton from the biggest and most ambitious agricultural irrigation scheme in Zimbabwe.

This scheme resulted from the drive and insight of one man, Thomas Murray MacDougall. His dream of turning the south east into one of the country's biggest agricultural areas survived many years of frustration and official discouragement before turning into reality.

By 1930, almost single handed, MacDougall had established his own irrigation scheme. He diverted the water of the Mtilikwe river through a 400 metre tunnel carved out of solid rock and into

a canal which led to his lands.

After many setbacks, he eventually discovered that sugarcane was one of the crops most suited to the climate and natural hazards of the region — and today's sugar industry was born.

As ofter happens, officialdom waited until the pioneering work had been done, and then stepped in to build the Kyle and Bangala dams and the 60km canal that brings water to much of the region.

Today, sugar and cotton are the mainstays of the region, although several other crops are grown as well. Sugar, in particular, has provided the raw material for one of Zimbabwe's biggest technological triumphs: the production of motor fuel from sugar cane.

A large processing plant produces ethanol, using techniques developed in Brazil and Germany. All petrol sold in Zimbabwe now has a 15 percent ethanol content.

Cotton, much of it grown by small farmers, is also an important lowveld crop and a ginnery has been set up to process the region's output.

Many parts of the lowveld that have not been cleared for the irrigation scheme are included in some of Zimbabwe's biggest cattle ranches.

However, modern thinking is turning more and more towards the ranching of local wildlife in order to make the best possible use of the veld and its resources of grazing and browsing.

Several landowners in the south east have pioneered wildlife ranching techniques that are recognised as among the best in the world.

With an area of 5 000sq. km, the remote and mysterious Gonarezhou is Zimbabwe's second largest national park.

It is cut by three of the country's biggest rivers. . In the northern end of the park the Save and Lunde run between granite hills for much of their course before converging deep in the wilderness close to the Mozambique border.

It is down here, at the Save-Lunde confluence, that ancient Arab mooring rings are rumoured to lie buried in the sands.

In the central part of the park the country becomes more gentle, except for his such as the remarkable Nyamtongwe that rise abruptly from seas of rolling bush.

Further south the Gonarezhou's third large river, the Mwenezi, meanders through areas such as Buffalo Bend and Malipati, where hundreds of wild animals gather during the dry season.

Most of Zimbabwe's more common species such as elephant, buffalo, hippo, impala, giraffe, zebra, kudu, eland and waterbuck are well represented within the park.

It is the home of some of Zimbabwe's biggest elephants. One of these, Kabakwe, has been given his own special conservation status by the government. Unlike other elephant, he may not be shot by hunters even if he strays out of the park and on to land where safaris are conducted.

Gonarezhou also harbours several less well-known species. Besides sable and roan it has one of Zimbabwe's only two populations of nyala antelope, concentrated around the Save-Lunde confluence; and fortunate visitors may also see oribi and Livingstone's suni.

The park also has a wide range of predators, including lion, leopard, hyaena, jackal, smaller cats — and even a few cheetah and wild dog.

Black rhinos were reintroduced into the Gonarezhou in the 1960's. Several animals were translocated from the Zambezi Valley and have since bred to form a small but nonetheless valuable population.

Much of the wildlife ranching activity in the south east borders on the Gonarezhou. Wild animals are able to move freely on to these ranches. Thus the park creates a central nucleus for modern techniques of wildlife utilisation.

It is possible to stand on the summits of the hills in the Gonarezhou and to see nothing but unbroken bush, extending to the horizon in every direction. Thus it forms a fitting completion to the story of the south east lowveld: a story of human endeavour, ancient and modern, typified by Great Zimbabwe and the huge irrigation schemes — and of the mystery, remoteness and plentiful wildlife in the distant reaches of Zimbabwe's second biggest national park.

The Eastern Highlands

THE EASTERN HIGHLANDS, yet another of Zimbabwe's fascinatingly diverse faces, often come as a surprise to visitors reared on the usual film and television portrayals of Africa.

There are no vast plains covered with herds of wildebeest; no wide rivers dotted with hippo and crocodiles; and no desert scrub with elephants jostling to drink at drying waterholes.

Instead, there is a 300 km chain of grassy downs, lush valleys and rugged mountains whose eastern walls often plunge hundreds of metres to the plains below.

Local peoples have lived within parts of the highlands for thousands of years. The Nyanga area in particular, with its plentiful stone ruins, ranks with Great Zimbabwe and the Matobo Hills as one of Zimbabwe's richest storehouses of history.

But the region as a whole also contains many national parks and botanical reserves whose diverse attractions range from the rain forests of the Vumba to the high, barren peaks of the Chimanimani mountains.

Travellers within the highlands can fish for trout in the cold fast-flowing streams and placid lakes, stroll through quiet, dark woodlands, see a surprising variety of animals in the wildlife sanctuaries, or simply marvel at the almost infinite variety of spectacular scenery.

And the keen naturalist will enjoy a particularly fruitful holiday as the highlands create refuges for many plants, birds and animals that cannot survive in the hotter, dryer parts of the country.

The Nyanga National Park, about 270km from Harare, is the most northerly of the conservation areas in the eastern highlands and is one of the most popular holiday spots in the country.

It was one of the first Zimbabwean national parks to achieve this status, and contains such dramatic features as Mount Inyangani, which at 2 592 metres is the country's highest mountain, and the beautiful Pungwe Falls

and Gorge.

Lying at altitudes generally ranging between 2 000 and 2 300 metres, much of the Nyanga area consists of lightly-vegetated downlands with long views and easy walking.

But Nyanga is also rich in pine forests, sparkling streams and tumbling waterfalls. Close to Nyanga village itself, a towering escarpment surmounted by the aptly-named World's View provides sweeping panoramas of the downs and the plains to the north.

Immediately adjoining the Nyanga national park — almost an extension of it — is the tiny Mtarazi National Park, the site of Zimbabwe's highest waterfall. Some 760 metres high, the falls descend in two stages over vertical cliffs into the Honde river valley.

The more intrepid may wish to climb the slopes of Inyangani. The effort is well rewarded by the splendour of the view from the summit — into Mocambique to the east and across Nyanga and into Zimbabwe in the west.

Local wildlife, though not as spectacular as that of Hwange or Mana Pools, is nonetheless both interesting and prolific. Though casual visitors are unlikely to see them, the record even includes occasional sightings of buffalo and lion.

Kudu, reedbuck, klipspringer, leopard, hyaena and many other species can be seen

within the park, but Nyanga is most noted for its populations of blue duiker and the rare samango monkey. Neither is found anywhere else in Zimbabwe.

The ruined stonemasonry of several cultures lies scattered across many of Nyanga's hills and plains. One of these cultures arrived in the area about 1 000 years ago. Before vanishing completely, they erected the structures that now lie in desolate but still impressive grandeur at Nyahokwe, just beyond the park's northern boundary.

They ultimately felt secure enough to descend to the lowlands, where they built what are now called the Van Niekerk ruins, which lie a few kilometres west of Nyahokwe and cover more than 80sq. km.

The eastern highlands are also one of Zimbabwe's major forestry areas and provide almost 80 percent of the country's softwood needs. Several large forest estates grow pines, eucalypts, poplars and cypresses.

The growing cycle of the pines is around 30 years. During this time the trees are pruned and thinned regularly. Mature logs from the forests are rough-sawn into boards, then kiln-dried and sent to factories in Mutare and Harare for processing into a wide range of products.

The biggest single consumer of pine in Zimbabwe is the building industry. It is followed by the packaging industry, which uses large quantities of timber in the manufacture of tobacco crates for export.

Many "one-off" types of packaging are also made from these softwoods, including, notably, the manufacture of crates in which Zimbabwean animals are sometimes sent abroad.

And some of the timber produced in the highlands is also used in the manufacture of pulp and paper.

Nestled in its valley in the heart of the eastern highlands, Mutare is one of the most attractively-sited cities in southern Africa.

With a population of some 70 000, it is the main commercial and industrial centre for the region. The manufacture of pulp and paper, carpets, and the assembly of motor vehicles are all numbered among Mutare's diverse activities.

The city also has direct road and rail links with Harare and is served by an airfield a few minutes from its centre.

Mutare lies a stone's throw from the magnificent Vumba National Park and also has its own nature reserve, Cecil Kop, on its northern boundary.

Inaugurated and run by the Wildlife Society of Zimbabwe, Cecil Kop contains a wide variety of local vegetation types, from montane grassland and evergreen forest to open msasa woodlands and grassy vleis.

The reserve contains many uncommon species including blue duiker, sun squirrels, samango monkeys, Gurney's sugarbirds, redfaced crimsonwings, grey waxbills and crowned eagles.

Part of the reserve has also been stocked with white rhinos, elephant, tsessebe, zebra, sable, wildebeest, giraffe, nyala, waterbuck, eland, impala and kudu.

One of Cecil Kop's main objectives is the education of young people concerning the need for natural resource conservation, and in particular of wildlife, soils and vegetation. Schools from all over Zimbabwe — and even from Europe on one or two occasions — visit the reserve. South of Mutare the road winds up into the Vumba mountains — the "mountains of mist", so named because of the early morning mists that often shroud their summits before dispersing under the rising sun.

Within the Vumba fertile soils and generous annual rains — over 1 500 mm on average — combine with the mists and sun to create a region of unparalleled lushness and verdancy.

An 80 hectare national park, containing thousands of plants, has been created in the midst of the Vumba.

It features wide, pleasant tracts of lawn, several artificial ponds

and a small lake fed by mountain streams that cascade over tiny waterfalls among the beds of flowering plants.

The Vumba contains virtually every local and exotic species of plant that will grow in the region. It has almost five thousand varieties of fuchsia; a similar number of azaleas; and 20 varieties of protea as well as aloes, exotic shrubs, bulbs and colourful annuals.

The park also has extensive areas of indigenous montane woodlands. In these woodlands, the high humidities encourage the growth of the fascinating

tree ferns, often hundreds of years old, and which may reach several metres in height.

Sheltered footpaths give access to every corner of the gardens and extend for 12 km through the woodlands.

The park follows the line of a stream along the eastern slope of the mountains. At its edge the ground falls away to give a magnificent view of the Mocambique plains, almost 1 000 metres below.

Minutes away from the Vumba National Park lies the Bunga Forest Reserve, which was specially constituted to protect the rare and endangered indigenous plants of the region.

Recently enlarged to encompass more than 1 500 hectares, the forest is a representative community of the flora found in the highlands.

Together with the Vumba National Park, it supports large numbers of butterflies, blue duiker and samango monkeys; and a wide range of bird life, with 130 known species recorded throughout the year.

Further south, the Vumba gives way to the stark and imposing Chimanimani mountains — without doubt the most striking mountain range in Zimbabwe.

Though only 50km in length, the range reaches 2 440 metres at its highest and presents peak after peak of austere granite rock rising majestically from wooded valleys containing lakes, marshes and streams. The 171sq km Chimanimani National Park includes virtually all of the range that lies within Zimbabwe. There are no roads into the mountains, although picturesque picnic sites in the foothills can be reached by car from the village of Chimanimani.

Amateur botanists will be particularly fascinated by the range and colours of the plants that thrive in the fine soils eroded from the mountainsides: cedarwoods, yellowwoods, ferns and tree and ground orchids.

But all who brave the mountains will discover a singularly lovely world of wide, windswept vistas and ageless grey-blue rock.

ZIMBABWE PORTRAIT